Your Colleagues Are Making More Than You?

A Guide on How to Know if You Are Underpaid at Work, and What to Do to Get More Money from Your Job

I have the distinct pleasure of introducing a book that is not only timely but also essential in our current economic climate: **"Your Colleagues Are Making More Than You**? A Guide on How to Know if You Are Underpaid at Work, and What to Do to Get More Money from Your Job."

In an era where the conversation about fair pay is louder than ever, this book serves as a beacon of knowledge and empowerment.

It is a comprehensive guide that peels back the curtain on the often-taboo subject of salary in the workplace.

With meticulous research and real-world examples, the book provides readers with the tools they need to determine if they are being underpaid and, more importantly, what actionable steps they can take to rectify this situation.

The book begins by exploring the psychological impact of discovering that one's colleagues are earning more. It delves into the feelings of frustration, demotivation, and the sense of injustice that can arise.

But it does not stop there. It goes on to equip the reader with a deep understanding of the factors that contribute to pay discrepancies.

From educational background, years of experience, to the subtleties of negotiating a salary, the book leaves no stone unturned.

One of the most valuable aspects of this guide is its emphasis on self-worth and advocacy. It encourages readers to reflect on their contributions to their workplace and to recognize the value they bring.

With this foundation, it then lays out a clear and strategic approach to discussing compensation with employers. The book stresses the importance of preparation, from gathering salary data to practicing negotiation techniques, ensuring that readers are fully equipped to enter these discussions with confidence.

Furthermore, "Your Colleagues Are Making More Than You?" addresses the broader implications of pay inequality and the importance of transparency in fostering a more equitable work environment. It calls for a cultural shift towards openness about salaries, which can lead to more fair and consistent compensation practices across the board.

In conclusion, this book is not just a guide; it is a catalyst for change. It empowers individuals to take control of their financial futures and encourages a dialogue that could lead to systemic change in the workplace. For anyone who has ever felt undervalued or underpaid, this book is must-read. It is a step towards a future where everyone is compensated fairly for their hard work and dedication.

Thank you for your attention, and I highly recommend picking up a copy of "Your Colleagues Are Making More Than You?" to anyone seeking to understand their worth and fight for the pay they deserve.

Welcome to the Salary Jungle

Have you ever stared at your paycheck, wondering if it is the financial equivalent of a "participation trophy"? Do you find yourself daydreaming about what life would be like if you had a few extra zeros in your bank account?

If you have ever suspected that your colleagues are making more than you, or if you are just curious about how to make more money from your job, you have picked up the right book.

The Office Salary Olympics

Let us face it: talking about money at work is like bringing up politics at a family dinner. It is awkward, uncomfortable, and can lead to heated debates.

But just because it is a touchy subject does not mean it is not important. Understanding your worth and ensuring you are compensated fairly is crucial to your professional and personal well-being.

And yes, your colleagues might be making more than you. But instead of sulking about it, let us turn that into motivation to get you what you deserve.

Why This Book?

This book is not just a dry manual filled with generic advice. It is a guide infused with humor and practical tips to help you navigate the often-confusing world of workplace compensation.

Whether you are a fresh graduate stepping into the workforce, a mid-career professional feeling stuck, or even a seasoned veteran wondering if you are still getting the best deal, this book has something for you.

Ready to Dive In?

So, if you are ready to stop wondering and start acting, let us dive in. By the end of this book, you will not only know if you are underpaid but also have a concrete plan to do something about it.

Whether it is through negotiating a raise, finding a new job, or leveraging your skills for better opportunities, you will be equipped with the knowledge and tools to boost your earning potential.

Grab your favorite beverage, settle into a comfy chair, and get ready to embark on a journey that could transform your professional life.

Because everyone deserves to be paid what they are worth – including you.

Welcome to "Your Colleagues Are Making More Than You: A Guide on How to Know if You Are Underpaid at Work, and What to Do to Get More Money from Your Job." Let us get started!

Table of Contents

Introduction

Chapter 1: Recognizing the Signs You're Underpaid

Chapter 2: Doing the Research

Chapter 3: Evaluating Your Own Worth

Chapter 4: Building Your Case

Chapter 5: Negotiation Strategies & aggressive negotiator

Chapter 6: Leveraging Offers

Chapter 7: Beyond Salary – Perks and Benefits

Chapter 8: When to Walk Away

Chapter 9: Continuous Self-Improvement & visualization

Conclusion & Lexicon

References on Negotiation skill in a work place

Introduction

Chapter 1: Recognizing the Signs You're Underpaid

The Coffee Machine Conundrum

You walk into the office, bleary-eyed from your morning commute. The fluorescent lights flicker overhead, and the smell of freshly brewed coffee wafts through the air. As you head toward the break room, you notice your colleagues huddled around the coffee machine, chatting, and laughing.

But something catches your eye—a subtle shift in their expressions when they glance at you. It is a mix of sympathy and guilt, as if they know something you do not.

The Coffee Machine Test

What if I told you that the coffee machine holds the key to unlocking the truth about your salary? It sounds absurd, but bear with me.

Imagine this scenario: You are standing in front of the coffee machine, waiting for your cup to fill. Your colleague, Sarah, joins you.

She has been at the company for about the same time as you, doing similar work. As you both sip your coffee, she casually mentions her recent raise. It is a significant bump—a number that makes your eyes widen.

Now, here is the conundrum: Do you ask her how much she is making? It is a delicate dance—one misstep, and you risk revealing your own salary or coming across as nosy.

But if you do not ask, you will never know if you are being underpaid.

Signs You Might Be Underpaid

The Coffee Machine Glances: Those sympathetic looks from your colleagues—they are not just in your head. People tend to avoid discussing salaries openly, but their expressions can give you clues.

If your coworkers seem uncomfortable when the topic comes up, it might be a sign that salaries are not equal across the board.

Comparing Notes: Pay attention during casual conversations. When coworkers discuss their weekend plans or recent purchases, listen for hints about their financial situations.

If they are taking lavish vacations or buying expensive gadgets, it could indicate they are earning more than you.

Job Postings and Industry Standards: Research job postings for similar roles in your industry.

Are the salary ranges significantly higher than what you are currently earning? If so, it is time to reassess.

Your Accomplishments vs. Compensation: Reflect on your achievements. Have you consistently exceeded expectations? If your performance merits recognition, but your paycheck does not reflect it, you might be underpaid.

Market Trends: Industries evolve, and so do compensation norms. Keep an eye on market trends.

If your salary has not kept pace with industry standards, it is a red flag.

What to Do Next

Gather Data: Arm yourself with information. Research salary benchmarks for your role, experience level, and location. Websites like Glassdoor and LinkedIn can provide valuable insights.

Have the Conversation: It is uncomfortable, but necessary. Approach your manager or HR with confidence.

Be prepared to discuss your accomplishments and present your case for a raise.

Know Your Worth: Remember that your value extends beyond your current paycheck. Consider benefits, work-life balance, and growth opportunities.

Conclusion

The coffee machine conundrum is more than just a quirky workplace scenario—it is a metaphor for recognizing your worth.

Do not settle for less; take charge of your financial future. And who knows? Maybe one day, you will be the one sipping coffee with a secret smile, knowing you have cracked the code.

Note: The characters and situations in this chapter are fictional.

I hope you find this chapter helpful! If you need further assistance or have any other requests, feel free to ask

The Car Comparison: Your colleagues are driving the latest models while you are still coaxing life out of your old beater.

The classic car comparison! It is like watching a parade of sleek, shiny vehicles while you are cruising along in your trusty old steed.

But fear not! There is a certain charm to driving an older car. It is like wearing a well-worn pair of jeans – comfortable, familiar, and full of memories. Plus, think of all the money you are saving on car payments and insurance premiums!

So, while your colleagues might be flaunting their high-tech gadgets and leather seats, just remember that your beater has character.

It is seen sunrises, road trips, and maybe even a few spilled coffee mishaps. And hey, who needs lane departure warnings when you have got that sixth sense for potholes?

Keep on coaxing life out of that old faithful – it has got stories to tell!

Remember to highlight negotiation strategies, market research, and the importance of advocating for fair compensation.

Chapter 2: Doing the Research

Salary Surveys and Tools

There is a wealth of resources out there to help you figure out what your job is worth. Websites like Glassdoor, PayScale, and LinkedIn Salary can give you a good idea of the average salary for your position in your location.

Salary Surveys

Industry Surveys: Look for industry-specific salary surveys. These provide average salaries based on roles, experience, and location.

Company-Specific Data: Some companies share salary data publicly. Check their annual reports or websites.

Professional Associations: Join relevant associations for access to salary data.

Online Platforms: Websites like Glassdoor, Payscale, indeed, and LinkedIn offer salary insights.

Tools for Research

Payscale: Compare your salary against industry averages.

Bureau of Labor Statistics (BLS): Government data on wages by occupation and region.

LinkedIn Salary Insights: Explore salary ranges for specific roles.

Job Boards: Analyze job postings to gauge salary expectations.

Remember, knowledge is power! Feel free to explore these resources and gather insights to advocate for fair compensation.

Industry Benchmarks

Join professional groups and networks. Sometimes the best information comes from talking to people in your industry at conferences, meetups, or even online forums.

Comparison and Context: Industry benchmarks allow you to gauge how well your business is doing compared to others in your field.

Whether it is customer satisfaction, product quality, or operational costs, having reference points helps you understand where you stand1.

Expanded Network: Joining professional groups and networks is essential.

These communities provide access to a broader network, facilitating meaningful connections and collaboration opportunities.

You will meet like-minded professionals and gain visibility.

Accelerated Development: Through networking, you discover courses, webinars, podcasts, and meetups that enhance your skills and industry knowledge. It is a fast track to professional development.

Visibility and Opportunities: Networking increases your visibility as an independent professional.

It puts you in front of potential collaborators, clients, and job opportunities. Referrals and recommendations often stem from strong community relationships.

So, attend those conferences, participate in meetups, and engage in online forums – your network can be a powerful asset!

Chapter 3: Evaluating Your Own Worth

Skill Assessment

Take a hard look at your skills and experience. Are you a master of spreadsheets, a wizard with code, or a marketing maven? List your key skills and accomplishments.

Here are 4 top skills:

[Advanced Excel proficiency](#) is a valuable skill that can significantly enhance your productivity and problem-solving abilities. Here are some areas where advanced Excel skills come into play:

Formulas and Functions:

Mastering complex formulas (e.g., VLOOKUP, INDEX-MATCH, SUMIFS) allows you to manipulate data efficiently.

Creating custom functions using VBA (Visual Basic for Applications) extends Excel's capabilities.

Data Analysis:

PivotTables: Summarize and analyze large datasets.

Data validation: Ensure data accuracy and consistency.

Conditional formatting: Highlight trends and outliers.

Automation:

Macros: Record repetitive tasks and automate them.

Customizing ribbons and shortcuts for quick access.

Visualizations:

Charts and graphs: Present data visually (bar charts, line graphs, scatter plots).

Sparklines: Tiny charts within cells for trend visualization.

Modeling and Simulation:

Goal Seek: Find input values to achieve desired results.

Scenario Manager: Test different scenarios based on changing variables.

Remember, Excel proficiency is not just about knowing the basics – it is about leveraging these advanced features to streamline your work

Effective communication:

is a critical skill in any professional setting. Here are some key aspects to consider:

Clarity: Express your ideas concisely and clearly. Avoid jargon or overly complex language.

Active Listening: Pay attention to others, ask questions, and show genuine interest.

Empathy: Understand different perspectives and adapt your communication style accordingly.

Nonverbal Communication: Body language, eye contact, and gestures matter.

Written Communication: Craft well-structured emails, reports, and memos.

Conflict Resolution: Address disagreements respectfully and find common ground.

Remember, effective communication is not just about what you say — it is about how you say it!

Project management is a multifaceted skill that involves planning, organizing, and executing tasks to achieve specific goals. Here are some key aspects:

Project Initiation:

Define project objectives, scope, and stakeholders.

Create a project charter or kickoff document.

Planning:

Develop a project plan with tasks, timelines, and dependencies.

Allocate resources (people, budget, equipment).

Risk assessment and mitigation planning.

Execution:

Coordinate team members.

Monitor progress and adjust as needed.

Address issues and changes.

Monitoring and Control:

Track project performance.

Manage scope creep.

Ensure quality standards are met.

Closure:

Evaluate project success.

Document lessons learned.

Celebrate achievements!

Negotiation skills are essential for achieving win-win outcomes. Here are some tips:

Preparation:

Research the situation, understand your goals, and anticipate the other party's position.

Know your value – what unique skills or contributions do you bring?

Active Listening:

Understand the other party's needs and concerns.

Ask open-ended questions to gather information.

How to be an active listener?

Limit Distractions:

During conversations, minimize distractions. Put away your phone, close unnecessary tabs, and focus on the speaker.

Show respect by giving your full attention.

Use Appropriate Body Language:

Maintain eye contact and nod to show engagement.

Avoid crossing your arms or looking disinterested.

Stay Present:

Be in the moment. Do not let your mind wander or plan your response while the other person is speaking.

Listen actively without interrupting.

Seek Meaning Later:

Understand that not every message is immediately clear. Sometimes meaning emerges as the conversation unfolds.

Be patient and open-minded.

Summarize What You Heard:

After the speaker finishes, paraphrase their main points. This shows you have truly understood.

Use phrases like, "So, if I understand correctly…"

Ask Follow-Up Questions:

Dig deeper by asking relevant questions. Clarify any ambiguities or explore related topics.

Show genuine interest in understanding their perspective.

Remember, active listening fosters better collaboration, reduces misunderstandings, and strengthens workplace relationships.

Assertiveness:

Clearly express your position and desired outcome.

Be respectful but firm.

Problem-Solving Mindset:

Focus on solutions, not just demands.

Explore creative options.

Flexibility:

Be willing to compromise without sacrificing your core needs.

Look for mutually beneficial solutions.

Performance Reviews - A Goldmine of Insights

Introduction

Performance reviews – those annual or semi-annual meetings that often induce a mix of anxiety and curiosity.

But fear not! These reviews are more than just a formality; they hold valuable clues about your professional journey.

In this chapter, we will explore why performance reviews matter, how to decode them, and how to leverage them to your advantage.

The Performance Review Ritual

1. **The Dreaded Email**

It arrives in your inbox: "Performance Review Scheduled."

Your heart races. Will it be praise or critique?

2. The Preparation

Dust off your memory. What did you achieve this year?

Gather evidence: project successes, client testimonials, metrics.

The Goldmine Within

1. The Ratings

The numerical or qualitative ratings exceeds expectations, meets expectations, needs improvement.

Decode them:

Exceeds Expectations: You are doing great! Keep it up.

Meets Expectations: Solid performance, but room for growth.

Needs Improvement: Uh-oh. Time for reflection.

2. The Comments

The heart of the review.

Look for patterns:

Specific Praise: Highlighted skills or accomplishments.

Constructive Criticism: Areas to work on.

Vague Statements: Decode these – what do they really mean?

3. The Goals

Future-oriented.

Set SMART goals (Specific, Measurable, Achievable, Relevant, Time-bound). Align them with your career aspirations.

Decoding the Subtext

1. The Tone

Friendly? Formal? Cold?

Tone reveals how your manager perceives you.

2. The Frequency

Regular reviews vs. sporadic ones.

Consistency matters.

3. The Timing

Before promotions or salary discussions.

A strategic move?

Leveraging Performance Reviews

1. Self-Reflection

What surprised you? What resonated?

Use feedback for growth.

2. Conversation Starters

Schedule a follow-up meeting.

Discuss specific feedback.

3. Negotiation Fuel

Highlight achievements during salary negotiations.

"In my last review, I consistently exceeded expectations."

The Art of Responding

1. Gratitude

Thank your manager for the feedback.

Show appreciation for growth opportunities.

2. Action Plan

Address areas for improvement. Share your goals.

Conclusion

Performance reviews are not just about ratings; they're about your professional evolution. So, dust off those reviews, mine the gold, and use them as steppingstones toward your career aspirations!

Performance ratings play a significant role in performance reviews at work. Let us explore their importance:

Evaluation and Feedback:

Performance ratings provide a structured way to evaluate an employee's performance.

They offer specific feedback on strengths, areas for improvement, and overall contributions.

Comparison and Differentiation:

Ratings allow managers to compare employees objectively.

High performers receive recognition, while low performers may need additional support.

Decision-Making:

Ratings inform decisions related to promotions, bonuses, and career development.

They help allocate resources effectively within the organization.

Transparency and Accountability:

Clear ratings create transparency. Employees understand where they stand.

Accountability increases when performance is quantified.

Remember, accurate and fair performance ratings contribute to a thriving workplace.

Chapter 4: Building Your Case

Documenting Achievements

Start compiling a list of your achievements. Think numbers, percentages, and dollar signs. The more quantifiable your accomplishments, the stronger your case.

Introduction

In the quest for fair compensation, building a strong case is essential. It is not enough to feel undervalued; you need evidence to support your claims. In this chapter, we will explore how to document your achievements effectively and present them convincingly.

The Importance of Documentation

1. Memory Fades

That project you rocked six months ago. It is a distant memory.

Documenting ensures you do not forget your wins.

2. Objective Evidence

When you say, "I'm great at X," your manager wants proof.

Documentation provides that proof.

What to Document

1. Quantifiable Achievements

Numbers Speak: Revenue generated, cost savings, deadlines met.

Before and After: Show the impact of your work.

2. Soft Skills

Client Testimonials: "Jane's communication skills saved our client relationship."

Team Collaboration: "John led a cross-functional team to success."

3. Projects and Initiatives

Project Descriptions: What did you lead? What challenges did you overcome?

Innovations: "Introduced automated reporting system, reducing manual work by 50%."

The Art of Documentation

1. Real-Time Notes

Daily Journal: Jot down wins, challenges, and lessons learned.

Email Folder: Save commendations and project updates.

2. Metrics Tracking

Excel or Google Sheets: Create a simple tracker.

Graphs and Charts: Visualize progress.

3. Visual Evidence

Screenshots: Before-and-after visuals.

Photos: Events, presentations, or completed projects.

Crafting Your Case

1. The **STAR** Method

    The STAR method is a structured technique used to answer behavioral interview questions. It stands for Situation, Task, Action, and Result. This approach allows the interviewee to provide clear, concise, and thoughtful answers based on real-life examples from their own experiences.

When using the STAR method, you break down your response into these four components:

Situation: Describe the context or situation you were in. What was the challenge or scenario you faced?
Task:
Explain the specific task or goal you needed to accomplish within that situation.

Action: Detail the actions you took to address the task. What steps did you follow? How did you approach the problem?

Result: Share the outcome of your actions. What happened because of your efforts? What impact did it have?

By using the STAR method, you can provide structured and compelling answers during interviews, showcasing your skills and demonstrating how you have handled similar situations in the past.
Remember to practice and tailor your responses to specific questions to make them shine bright!

2. Storytelling

Narrative: Weave your achievements into a compelling story.

Emphasize Growth: Show how you've evolved.

Presenting Your Case

1. Performance Reviews

Include Documentation: Do not rely solely on memory.

2. Salary Negotiations

Data + Achievements: "Based on industry standards and my accomplishments..."

Confidence: Present your case assertively.

Conclusion

Building your case is not about bragging; it is about advocating for your worth. Document your achievements diligently, and when the time comes, present them confidently.

Remember, you are not just asking for more money; you are asking for recognition

Testimonials and Recommendations

Gather recommendations from colleagues, managers, and clients. These can provide a solid backing to your claims.

Chapter 5: Negotiation Strategies

The Art of Negotiation

Practice your pitch. Consider role-playing with a trusted friend or mentor. Remember, confidence is key.

Research and Preparation:

Before any negotiation, gather data on industry standards, company benchmarks, and salary ranges for your role.

Websites like Glassdoor, Payscale, indeed, and LinkedIn can provide valuable insights.

Understand your own value by assessing your skills, experience, and contributions. What unique strengths do you bring to the table?

Timing Matters:

Choose the right moment to discuss salary. Ideally, wait until after you have received a job offer or during performance reviews.

<u>Be patient and avoid rushing into negotiations</u>. Gather evidence and build your case.

Know Your Desired Salary Range:

Determine the minimum acceptable salary (your "walk-away" point) and your ideal salary.

Aim for the higher end of the range but be realistic based on market conditions and your qualifications.

Focus on Value, Not Need:

Frame your negotiation around the value you bring to the organization. Highlight your accomplishments, skills, and potential impact.

Avoid discussing personal financial needs or hardships.

<u>Practice</u> **Active Listening:**

Understand the employer's perspective. What are their priorities? What challenges do they face?

Listen carefully during the negotiation to identify areas where you can align your interests with theirs.

Use the Power of Silence:

After stating your desired salary, pause. Let the other party respond.

Silence can be uncomfortable but powerful. It encourages the other party to make concessions.

Leverage Non-Salary Benefits:

If the base salary is not negotiable, explore other perks: bonuses, stock options, flexible work hours, remote work, health benefits, and professional development opportunities.

Consider the total compensation package, not just the base pay.

Be Confident and Assertive:

Maintain eye contact, speak clearly, and express your points confidently.

Use phrases like "I believe my skills warrant a higher salary" rather than "I hope you can consider…"

Practice Role-Playing:

Enlist a friend or mentor to simulate the negotiation. Practice different scenarios.

Gain confidence by rehearsing your responses.

Be Prepared to Walk Away:

Sometimes negotiations do not yield the desired outcome. Be ready to decline an offer if it falls significantly short.

Remember that your worth extends beyond any single job opportunity.

Remember, negotiation is a skill that improves with practice. Be respectful, professional, and open-minded throughout the process.

Good luck, and may your negotiations be fruitful!

How to deal with an aggressive negotiator:

Dealing with aggressive or uncooperative negotiators can be challenging, but there are effective strategies to navigate such situations. Here are some tips:

Stay Calm and Composed:

Maintain your composure even if the other party becomes aggressive.

Avoid reacting emotionally or escalating the tension.

Listen Actively:

Understand their perspective. Sometimes aggression stems from frustration or fear.

Show empathy and acknowledge their feelings.

Set Boundaries:

Be assertive but respectful. Clearly state what behavior is unacceptable.

For example, you can say, "I understand your frustration, but let's keep the conversation professional."

Focus on Interests, Not Positions:

Look beyond their aggressive stance. Identify their underlying interests.

Find common ground and explore win-win solutions.

Use the "Feel, Felt, Found" Technique:

Acknowledge their emotions: "I understand how you feel."

Share a similar experience: "Others have felt the same way."

Transition to a positive outcome: "What they found helpful was…"

Redirect the Conversation:

Shift the focus to the issues at hand. Reframe the discussion.

For example, "Let's focus on finding a solution to the problem."

Be Patient and Persistent:

Aggressive behavior may be a negotiation tactic. Do not give up.

Keep the lines of communication open and seek common ground.

Remember, maintaining professionalism and seeking mutual understanding can lead to better outcomes, even with difficult negotiators

Chapter 6: Leveraging Offers

Job Offers

If you are interviewing elsewhere and receive an offer, it can be a powerful tool in your negotiation arsenal.

Just be careful not to bluff unless you are prepared to walk away.

When you receive a job offer, it is an opportunity to negotiate not only the terms of that specific offer but also to use it as leverage for your current position or other potential opportunities. Here is how to maximize your leverage:

Understand Your Market Value:

Before leveraging an offer, ensure you know your market value. Research industry standards, salary ranges, and benefits for your role.

Use tools like Glassdoor, LinkedIn, and salary surveys to gather data.

Receive the Offer in Writing:

Always request a written offer. This provides clarity and ensures you have all the details.

Once you have it, express gratitude and take time to review it thoroughly.

Evaluate the Offer Holistically:

Look beyond just the base salary. Consider bonuses, stock options, benefits, vacation days, and other perks.

Calculate the total compensation package to understand its true value.

Assess Your Current Situation:

Evaluate your current job, including your salary, responsibilities, and growth prospects.

Identify areas where your current role falls short or where you'd like improvement.

Schedule a Meeting with Your Manager:

How to prepare for a meeting with your manager?

Reflect on Your Goals:

Think about what aspects of your job bring you fulfillment and success.

Consider how you want your daily workday to look and what career aspirations you have1.

Research Opportunities:

Investigate career growth opportunities within your company.

Understand the available advancement paths and leadership positions1.

Know Your Value:

Be confident in expressing your contributions to the team or organization.

Advocate for yourself by highlighting your successes, knowledge, and leadership abilities.

Then, Request a Meeting:

Schedule a dedicated meeting with your manager specifically to discuss your career growth.

Avoid folding this conversation into routine one-on-one meetings or performance reviews.

Articulate Your Insights:

Clearly express your goals and interests during the meeting.

Share how you add value and how you envision your future within the company.

How to create a Forward-Looking Plan:

Set Clear Goals:

Define your short-term and long-term objectives. What do you want to achieve in the next 6 months, 1 year, or 5 years?

Ensure your goals align with your personal aspirations and the company's vision.

Assess Your Skills and Gaps:

Identify the skills needed to reach your goals.

Evaluate your current skill set. What areas require improvement or development?

Create a Skill Development Plan:

Break down the skills into manageable chunks.

Set deadlines for acquiring or enhancing each skill.

Consider formal training, online courses, or mentorship.

Build Relationships:

Networking is essential for career growth.

Connect with colleagues, industry professionals, and mentors.

Attend conferences, workshops, and industry events.

Seek Feedback Regularly:

Request feedback from your manager, peers, and team members.

Use constructive criticism to refine your approach.

Stay Informed:

Keep up with industry trends, technological advancements, and market shifts.

Read relevant articles, follow thought leaders, and subscribe to newsletters.

Map Out Milestones:

Create a timeline with milestones for achieving your goals.

Celebrate small victories along the way.

Be Adaptable:

Plans may change due to unforeseen circumstances.

Be flexible and adjust your plan as needed.

Remember, a forward-looking plan is dynamic—it evolves as you grow and learn. Stay committed, stay curious, and keep moving forward!

After the meeting, draft a plan outlining next steps:

Identify new skills you need to acquire.

Specify projects you have agreed to take on.

Consider building relationships with important stakeholders.

Remember, <u>proactive communication</u> about your future goals demonstrates your commitment and helps align your career trajectory with organizational needs

Be transparent with your manager. Explain that you have received an offer and would like to discuss it.

Frame the conversation positively: "I've been presented with an exciting opportunity…"

Present the Offer Professionally:

Share the key details of the offer with your manager. Be factual and concise.

Highlight the aspects that are attractive and relevant to your current situation.

Express Your Interest in Staying:

Emphasize your commitment to the company and your desire to continue contributing.

Mention specific achievements and your dedication to the team.

Propose Improvements:

Based on your research and the offer, propose specific changes to your current compensation.

Be prepared to negotiate not only salary but also other benefits.

Be Open to Counteroffers:

Your manager may counter with an improved offer. Be receptive and considerate.

If the counteroffer is acceptable, express your gratitude and acceptance.

Know When to Walk Away:

Sometimes leveraging an offer does not yield the desired outcome.

If your current employer is not willing to meet your expectations, be prepared to accept the external offer.

Remember, leverage is not about threatening to leave; it's about advocating for your worth. Approach negotiations professionally, maintain positive relationships, and make informed decisions. Leverage wisely, and may your career thrive!

Internal Opportunities

Sometimes the best move is within your current company. Look for opportunities to move up or laterally into a higher-paying role.

Promotions:

Seek promotions within your current department or team. A promotion typically involves moving to a higher-level position with increased responsibilities and often a higher salary.

Demonstrate your skills, take on additional tasks, and express your interest in growth to your supervisor.

Lateral Moves:

Consider lateral moves to different roles or departments. These moves may not necessarily be upward but can provide valuable experience and exposure.

Lateral moves can broaden your skill set and make you more versatile.

Transfers:

Explore opportunities in other branches or locations of your company. Transfers allow you to experience different work environments and cultures.

Be open to relocation if necessary.

Special Projects and Task Forces:

Participate in cross-functional projects or task forces. These initiatives often involve collaboration with colleagues from various departments.

Exposure to different areas can enhance your skills and visibility.

Job Rotation Programs:

Some companies offer formal job rotation programs. These allow employees to move through different roles over a defined period.

Job rotations can provide a holistic understanding of the organization.

Skill Development:

Attend workshops, training sessions, and conferences. Acquire new skills that align with your career goals.

Showcase your continuous learning to stand out.

Networking and Mentoring:

Build relationships with colleagues, managers, and senior leaders. Networking can lead to internal opportunities.

Seek mentors who can guide your career path.

Monitor Job Postings Internally:

Regularly check your company's internal job board. New positions may open.

Apply strategically based on your interests and qualifications.

Express Your Ambitions:

Communicate your career aspirations to your supervisor. Discuss your desire for growth and ask for guidance.

Be proactive in seeking feedback and discussing your development plan.

Stay Positive and Patient:

Internal opportunities may take time. Stay committed and maintain a positive attitude.

Remember that persistence pays off.

What if the other party's aggression affects my confidence during negotiation?

Dealing with an aggressive counterpart can indeed impact your confidence during negotiations.

Available on Amazon

Here are some strategies to maintain your composure and regain confidence:

Self-Awareness:

Recognize your emotional reactions. Understand that their aggression is not a reflection of your worth or abilities.

Remind yourself that you are prepared and capable.

Positive Self-Talk:

Counter negative thoughts with positive affirmations.

For example, "I am well-prepared," "I have valuable insights," or "I can handle this."

Focus on Facts and Objectives:

Shift your attention away from their behavior. Concentrate on the negotiation's purpose and your goals.

Ground yourself in the facts and the desired outcome.

Breathe and Regulate Stress:

Take deep breaths to calm your nervous system.

Practice mindfulness techniques to stay centered.

Use Assertive Language:

Choose your words carefully. Be assertive without being aggressive.

For instance, "I appreciate your passion, but let's focus on finding common ground."

Visualize Success:

Imagine a positive outcome. Visualize yourself confidently handling the situation.

Visualization can boost self-assurance.

Seek Support:

Reach out to a mentor, friend, or coach. Discuss your feelings and gain perspective.

External validation can bolster your confidence.

Remember, their aggression is about them, not you. Stay resilient, stay professional, and trust in your abilities

Chapter 7: Beyond Salary – Perks and Benefits

Total Compensation Package

Salary is important, but do not overlook benefits like health insurance, retirement plans, stock options, and more.

Health Insurance:

Comprehensive health coverage is essential. Evaluate the quality of medical, dental, and vision plans. Consider factors like premiums, deductibles, and coverage for dependents.

Retirement Plans:

Employer-sponsored retirement plans (such as 401(k) or RRSP) allow you to save for the future. Look for employer matching contributions and vesting schedules.

Paid Time Off (PTO):

Assess vacation days, sick leave, and holidays. A healthy work-life balance is crucial. Some companies offer additional perks like paid parental leave or sabbaticals.

Flexible Work Arrangements – Remote Work:

Explore options like remote work, flexible hours, or compressed workweeks.

Flexibility can improve job satisfaction and productivity.

Remote Work:

Employees work from a location other than the office (e.g., home, co-working space).

Requires reliable internet access and self-discipline.

Benefits include reduced commuting time and increased work-life balance.

Flextime:

Allows employees to choose their start and end times within certain limits. For example, you might work 7:00 AM to 3:00 PM instead of the standard 9:00 AM to 5:00 PM.

Compressed Workweeks:

Condenses the workweek into fewer days (e.g., four 10-hour days instead of five 8-hour days). Provides longer weekends and can improve productivity.

Job Sharing:

Two employees split the responsibilities of a full-time role.

Each works part-time (e.g., three days a week) and shares information seamlessly.

Phased Retirement:

Allows older employees to gradually reduce their hours before retirement.

Helps retain institutional knowledge and provides a smoother transition.

Summer Hours:

Common in some industries during summer months. Employees work longer hours Monday to Thursday and have a shorter Friday.

Results-Only Work Environment (ROWE):

Focuses on outcomes rather than hours worked. Employees have autonomy to manage their time as long as they meet goals.

Parental Leave and Return-to-Work Programs:

Support parents by offering extended leave or gradual return options. Helps balance work and family responsibilities.

Flexibility for Personal Needs:

Accommodate personal appointments, family emergencies, or other life events. Trust-based systems allow employees to manage their time responsibly.

Customized Arrangements:

Some companies tailor flexible arrangements to individual needs.

<u>Discuss options with your manager and HR.</u>

Bonuses and Incentives:

Beyond base salary, inquire about performance-based bonuses, commissions, or profit-sharing.

Understand the criteria for earning these incentives.

Stock Options and Equity:

Stock options allow you to buy company shares at a predetermined price.

Equity grants align your interests with the company's success.

Professional Development:

Look for opportunities for skill development, certifications, and workshops.

Some employers offer tuition reimbursement or sponsor conferences.

Wellness Programs:

Wellness initiatives promote physical and mental health. Examples include gym memberships, counseling services, and stress management programs.

Transportation Benefits:

Commuter benefits (such as transit passes or parking subsidies) can save you money.

Evaluate the convenience and cost-effectiveness.

Employee Assistance Programs (EAP):

EAPs provide confidential counseling and support for personal or work-related issues.

Know how to access these services if needed.

Perks and Discounts:

Some companies offer discounts on products, services, or entertainment.

Explore employee perks like gym discounts, travel deals, or free meals.

Work-Life Balance

Sometimes a flexible schedule or remote work options can be worth more than a higher salary.

Company Culture:

Culture refers to the shared beliefs, behaviors, and norms within an organization.

It encompasses how people interact, communicate, and collaborate. A positive culture fosters employee engagement, satisfaction, and productivity. Examples of cultural aspects include teamwork, transparency, work-life balance, and inclusivity.

Values:

Values represent the core principles that guide decision-making and behavior. Companies often define their values explicitly (e.g., integrity, innovation, customer focus).

Employees who align with these values tend to thrive within the organization. Values influence everything from hiring to strategic planning.

Impact on Employees:

A strong culture and clear values create a sense of purpose and identity. Employees feel motivated when their personal values align with those of the company.

Conversely, a toxic culture can lead to burnout, turnover, and dissatisfaction.

Assessing Culture and Values:

Research the company's mission statement, website, and employee testimonials. Observe interactions during interviews or company events. Ask current employees about their experiences.

Cultural Diversity:

Embrace diversity in all its forms (ethnicity, gender, age, etc.).

Inclusive cultures value different perspectives and promote equity. Diversity enhances creativity and problem-solving.

Leadership's Role:

Leaders set the tone for culture and values. Their actions, communication, and decisions shape the organization. Transparent, ethical leadership fosters trust.

Chapter 8: When to Walk Away

Knowing when to leave a job or opportunity is crucial for your career and well-being. Here are some signs it might be time to walk away:

Unethical practices in the workplace can significantly impact employees and the organization.

Here are some examples of unethical behavior to watch out for:

Dishonesty and Fraud:

Falsifying records, misrepresenting information, or intentionally deceiving others. This erodes trust and damages the company's reputation.

Discrimination and Harassment:

Treating employees unfairly based on race, gender, religion, or other protected characteristics. A toxic environment can result from discrimination or harassment.

Bribery and Kickbacks:

Accepting or offering bribes, kickbacks, or other illegal incentives. These actions compromise integrity and violate laws.

Conflict of Interest:

When personal interests interfere with professional duties. Transparency is crucial to avoid conflicts.

Insider Trading:

Using non-public information to gain an advantage in stock trading.

This is illegal and unethical.

Exploitation:

Taking advantage of vulnerable employees (e.g., unpaid overtime, unsafe conditions). Fair treatment is essential.

Available on Amazon

Plagiarism and Intellectual Property Theft:

Copying others' work without proper attribution or stealing intellectual property. Respect original creators and their rights.

Environmental Violations:

Ignoring environmental regulations or causing harm to the environment.

Responsible practices benefit everyone.

Lack of Transparency:

Withholding information from employees or stakeholders.

Transparency builds trust.

Ignoring Safety Protocols:

Prioritizing profits over employee safety.

Safety should always come first.

Toxic Work Environment:

If the workplace is consistently negative, toxic, or harmful, it's time to move on.

Your mental and emotional health matter.

Stagnation:

If you have hit a career plateau with no growth prospects, explore new opportunities.

Lack of Recognition or Appreciation:

Feeling undervalued? If your efforts go unnoticed, it is time to evaluate. You deserve recognition for your hard work.

Burnout:

Chronic stress, exhaustion, and lack of work-life balance signal burnout. Prioritize your well-being.

Mismatched Goals:

If your personal and professional goals no longer align with the company's, reassess. You should feel passionate about your work.

Financial Instability:

If the company faces financial troubles or instability, consider your own security. Job security matters.

Health Issues:

If work negatively impacts your health (physical or mental), prioritize self-care. <u>Your health matters most.</u>

Lack of Learning Opportunities:

If you are not growing or learning, seek a more fulfilling environment.

Lifelong learning is essential.

Trust Your Gut:

Sometimes intuition tells you it's time to move on. Trust it.

Listen to your inner compass.

Remember, leaving is not failure—it's a strategic decision for your future.

Knowing Your Worth

Understanding your worth in the workplace is essential for career satisfaction and financial well-being. Here are some steps to help you assess your value:

Research Industry Standards:

Investigate salary ranges for your role in your industry and location.

Websites like Glassdoor, Payscale, indeed, and LinkedIn provide valuable data.

Evaluate Your Skills and Experience:

Be honest about your qualifications, expertise, and unique contributions.

Consider your education, certifications, and years of experience.

Track Your Achievements:

Keep a record of your accomplishments, projects, and positive outcomes.

Quantify results whenever possible (e.g., "Increased sales by 20%").

Understand Your Total Compensation:

Beyond salary, consider benefits, bonuses, and stock options.

Calculate the entire package to assess its value.

Assess Market Demand:

Is your skill set in high demand? Are there shortages in your field?

Scarcity often drives higher compensation.

Factor in Cost of Living:

Compare salaries based on the cost of living in your area.

Adjust expectations accordingly.

Be Prepared to Negotiate:

When discussing compensation, be confident and assertive.

Practice negotiation scenarios with a friend or mentor.

Remember that your worth extends beyond monetary compensation. Consider work-life balance, growth opportunities, and alignment with your values.

Advocate for what you deserve!

The Exit Strategy - Assess Your Reasons:

Why are you considering an exit? Is it dissatisfaction, career growth, or personal circumstances?

Understand your motivations to make an informed decision.

Evaluate Timing:

Consider the right time to exit. Is it after completing a project, during a performance review, or when a better opportunity arises?

Avoid abrupt departures if possible.

Financial Preparedness:

Assess your financial situation. Do you have savings to cover expenses during the transition?

Consider severance packages, unused vacation days, and any outstanding payments.

Update Your Resume and LinkedIn Profile:

Keep your professional profiles up to date.

Highlight your achievements and skills.

Network and Seek Opportunities:

Connect with colleagues, mentors, and industry contacts.

Explore job boards, attend networking events, and apply strategically.

Resign Professionally:

Schedule a meeting with your supervisor to discuss your decision.

Be respectful, express gratitude, and provide adequate notice (usually two weeks).

Knowledge Transfer:

Document your work processes, ongoing projects, and critical information.

Ensure a smooth handover to your successor.

Emotional Preparation:

Acknowledge Your Feelings:

Recognize any emotions you are experiencing—whether excitement, anxiety, or sadness.

It is normal to feel a mix of emotions during transitions.

Reflect on Your Journey:

Consider your achievements, growth, and the impact you've made.

Celebrate your successes and learn from challenges.

Visualize the Future:

Imagine the positive aspects of your next step.

Visualize your goals and the opportunities ahead.

Seek Support:

Talk to friends, family, or a mentor. Share your feelings and concerns.

Emotional support is essential during transitions.

Practice Self-Care:

Prioritize self-care: rest, exercise, and engage in activities you enjoy.

Manage stress and maintain balance.

Stay Open-Minded:

Embrace uncertainty as an opportunity for growth.

Be open to new experiences and connections.

Express Gratitude:

Appreciate the people, experiences, and lessons from your current situation.

Gratitude helps ease transitions.

Remember that emotions are valid, and it's okay to feel a mix of excitement and apprehension. Trust yourself and may this transition lead to positive outcomes!

Leaving can be emotional. Mentally prepare for the transition.

Focus on the positive aspects of your next step.

Stay Professional Until the End:

Maintain a positive attitude, even during your notice period.

Exit gracefully, leaving a positive impression.

Complete Your Responsibilities: Finish pending tasks, meet deadlines, and ensure a smooth transition for your team.

Positive Attitude: Stay positive and approachable. Avoid negativity or gossip.

Thank Colleagues: Express gratitude to coworkers and supervisors. Acknowledge their contributions.

Document Processes: Create clear instructions for your replacement. Share knowledge generously.

Stay Engaged: Attend meetings, participate actively, and contribute until your last day.

Say Goodbyes: Farewell emails or small gatherings can be a nice way to say goodbye.

Remember, leaving on a positive note reflects well on your professionalism and integrity.

Chapter 9: Continuous Self-Improvement

Skills Development

The importance of skills development:

Lifelong Learning:

Commit to learning throughout your career. Attend workshops, take courses, and read relevant books.

Stay curious and adapt to changing trends.

Soft Skills:

Develop communication, teamwork, and leadership skills.

Emotional intelligence, adaptability, and empathy are equally crucial.

Technical Skills:

Stay updated in your field. Learn new programming languages, tools, or methodologies.

Master the skills that align with your role.

Networking:

Build professional relationships. Attend conferences, join industry groups, and connect on LinkedIn.

Networking opens doors to opportunities.

Time Management:

Efficiently manage your time. Prioritize tasks, set goals, and avoid procrastination.

Time management enhances productivity.

Feedback and Reflection:

Seek feedback from colleagues, mentors, and supervisors.

Reflect on your performance and identify areas for improvement.

Adaptability:

Embrace change. Be open to new challenges and technologies.

Adaptability ensures long-term success.

Remember, continuous self-improvement is a journey. Invest in yourself—it pays dividends!

Never stop learning. Invest in courses, certifications, and training to keep your skills sharp and in demand.

Networking

Build and maintain a strong professional network. The more connections you have, the more opportunities will come your way.

Why Networking Matters

Beyond the Resume: Networking goes beyond submitting applications and relying solely on your resume. It leverages personal and business connections to create opportunities.

Insider Insights: Employers often hire through referrals. Having contacts within their network provides valuable insights into your qualities and fit.

Access to Hidden Jobs: Many positions are not publicly advertised. Networking opens doors to these hidden job opportunities.

Get Face-to-Face:

While online networking is convenient, in-person interactions are powerful. Schedule lunches or coffee meetings with industry professionals.

Attend industry-specific conventions, job fairs, and business-hosted events. Meet new people and exchange business cards.

Offer Help:

Networking is not just about taking; it's about giving. Help, share knowledge, and be genuinely interested in others' success.

Be a resource for your contacts, and they will remember you when opportunities arise.

Fight Your Fear:

Networking can be intimidating, especially for introverts. Remember that everyone starts somewhere.

Practice smart conversation starters and gradually build your confidence.

Be Patient and Make Time:

Networking takes time. Cultivate relationships over weeks or months.

Consistency matters—regularly attend events and follow up with contacts.

Emphasize Relationship-Building:

Networking is not transactional. Focus on building genuine relationships.

Show interest in others' careers, listen actively, and find common ground.

Use Social Networks and Online Resources:

Leverage platforms like LinkedIn. Connect with professionals in your field.

Participate in industry-specific forums and discussion boards.

Follow Up:

After meeting someone, send a personalized follow-up email. Express gratitude and mention specific points from your conversation.

Nurture relationships by staying in touch periodically.

Maximizing Online Networking

LinkedIn: Optimize your LinkedIn profile. Join relevant groups, participate in discussions, and connect with industry peers.

Online Forums: Visit job-related forums (like Indeed.com Job Forums) to engage with professionals and seek advice.

Attend Industry Events

Conferences and Expositions: Attend industry-specific events. These gatherings offer networking opportunities and educational sessions.

Continuing Education Forums: Explore workshops, seminars, and webinars. Connect with experts and fellow learners.

Networking Etiquette

Be Professional: Dress appropriately, maintain eye contact, and offer a firm handshake.

Elevator Pitch: Craft a concise pitch about yourself and your career goals.

Follow Up Promptly: Send thank-you notes after networking events.

Maintain Your Network

Stay Engaged: Regularly check in with your contacts. Share updates and celebrate their achievements.

Reciprocity: Be willing to help others when they seek advice or connections.

Overcoming Common Networking Challenges

Introversion: Practice small steps, like attending smaller events first.

Time Constraints: Allocate time for networking—it is an investment in your future.

Rejection: Not every connection will lead to a job offer. Do not take it personally; keep networking.

Remember, networking is not just about finding a job—it's about building lasting relationships that benefit both you and your professional community.

Visualize Success:

Visualizing success at work is a powerful technique that can positively impact your mindset and outcomes.

Here are some effective methods to help you visualize success:

Create a Vision Board:

Compile images, quotes, and symbols that represent your career goals.

Arrange them on a board or digital platform to create a visual reminder of your aspirations.

Write Down Your Goals:

Put your goals in writing. Be specific and detailed.

Describe what success looks like for you and how you'll achieve it.

Embrace Available Resources:

Recognize the tools, skills, and support systems at your disposal.

Visualize yourself utilizing these resources effectively.

Journal:

Write about your future achievements as if they have already happened.

Describe the emotions, experiences, and impact of your success.

Meditate:

Practice mindfulness meditation.

Envision yourself accomplishing your goals during meditation sessions.

Visualize Your Plan in Action:

Close your eyes and vividly imagine each step of your success journey.

See yourself overcoming challenges, making decisions, and celebrating achievements3.

Connect with Like-Minded People:

Surround yourself with colleagues, mentors, or friends who share your vision.

Discuss your goals and visualize collective success.

Remember, visualization is not just wishful thinking—it's a powerful tool to align your mindset with your desired outcomes

Conclusion

As we close this chapter, it is crucial to recognize that knowledge is power. Understanding the multifaceted reasons behind wage differences is the first step toward empowerment.

Whether these disparities are due to tenure, qualifications, negotiation skills, or systemic issues like the gender wage gap, each factor plays a critical role in the broader narrative of workplace compensation.

The book has underscored the importance of self-advocacy and the courage to initiate difficult conversations about pay.

It has also highlighted the value of market research and the necessity of approaching these discussions armed with data and a clear understanding of one is worth.

Moreover, "Your Coworkers Are Making More Money Than You" has shed light on the cultural shift towards transparency in the workplace.

This movement has the potential to dismantle long-standing inequities and pave the way for a more equitable distribution of wealth within our professional spheres.

In conclusion, while the revelation that your coworkers are making more money than you can be disheartening, it is not the end of the story. It is an invitation to reflect, to question, and to act. It is a call to advocate for oneself and for others, to strive for fairness, and to never settle for less than one is due.

As we turn the final page, let us carry forward the lessons learned and the resolve to seek a workplace where merit and fairness are not just ideals, but realities for all.

Lexicon (job negotiation skill)

lexicon of negotiation skills specifically relevant to job-related scenarios. These skills are essential for successful career growth and effective communication during negotiations:

Communication Skills:

Definition: The ability to express yourself clearly, persuasively, and engagingly.

Importance: Effective communication ensures mutual understanding, minimizes misunderstandings, and facilitates compromise.

Tips: Practice active listening, adapt your communication style to the listener, and use both verbal and nonverbal cues.

Active Listening:

Definition: The skill of fully engaging with the speaker, understanding their perspective, and recalling specific details.

Importance: Active listening helps you grasp the other party's needs, concerns, and goals.

Tips: Maintain eye contact, nod to show engagement, and avoid interrupting.

Emotional Intelligence:

Definition: The ability to recognize and manage your emotions and understand others' feelings.

Importance: Emotional intelligence keeps negotiations constructive, even during tense moments.

Tips: Stay calm, acknowledge emotions, and take breaks if needed.

Expectation Management:

Definition: Balancing your own expectations with those of the other party.

Importance: Realistic expectations prevent disappointment and allow for productive negotiations.

Tips: Be firm yet collaborative, adjusting expectations, as necessary.

Problem-Solving Skills:

Definition: The capacity to analyze complex situations, identify solutions, and find common ground.

Importance: Effective problem-solving leads to win-win outcomes.

Tips: Brainstorm creative solutions, consider alternatives, and focus on shared interests1.

Flexibility and Adaptability:

Definition: The willingness to adjust your approach based on changing circumstances.

Importance: Being adaptable allows you to navigate unexpected challenges.

Tips: Be open-minded, explore different paths, and be willing to compromise.

Preparation and Research:

Definition: Gathering relevant information about the negotiation context, the other party, and your own goals.

Importance: Preparedness boosts confidence and informs your strategy.

Tips: Research market standards, understand industry trends, and anticipate potential objections1.

Assertiveness:

Definition: Expressing your needs and advocating for your position without being aggressive.

Importance: Assertiveness ensures your voice is heard and prevents being taken advantage of.

Tips: Use "I" statements, be confident, and stand your ground respectfully.

Patience and Persistence:

Definition: Maintaining composure and staying committed throughout the negotiation process.

Importance: Patience prevents rash decisions, while persistence shows your dedication.

Tips: Be patient during impasses, take breaks if necessary, and keep the dialogue going.

Networking and Relationship Building:

Definition: Cultivating professional connections and building rapport.

Importance: Networking provides access to opportunities and potential allies.

Tips: Attend industry events, connect on LinkedIn, and nurture relationships over time.

Remember, negotiation skills are not only about getting what you want; they are about finding mutually beneficial solutions.

Mastering these skills enhances your career prospects and empowers you to navigate job-related negotiations successfully.

Here are some valuable resources on negotiation skills in the workplace:

Indeed.com: 12 Important Negotiation Skills

This article covers 12 essential negotiation skills, including communication, active listening, emotional intelligence, and expectation management1.

Harvard Business Review: Become a Better, Stronger, and More Confident Negotiator

Explore core principles for improving your negotiation skills, including framing for gain, preparation, timing, and making the ask2

Atlassian Work Life: How to Improve Your Negotiation Skills

Discover six research-backed best practices to feel more confident during negotiations and achieve better outcomes3.

Harvard Business School Online: 6 Negotiation Skills All Professionals Can Benefit From

Learn about six essential negotiation skills and ways to develop your knowledge and confidence4.

Remember to explore these resources to enhance your negotiation abilities and thrive in your workplace interactions!

Thank you for reading, and good luck on your journey to earning what you are worth!

Available on Amazon

©Photolator Editor 2024

www.ingramcontent.com/pod-product-compliance
Lightning Source LLC
Chambersburg PA
CBHW071953210526
45479CB00003B/915